The Life and Prayers of
Saint Anthony of Padua
Wyatt North

Wyatt North Publishing

About Wyatt North Publishing

Wyatt North Publishing is a boutique publishing company. We always provide high quality, perfectly formatted, Books.

We guarantee our Books. If you are not 100% satisfied we will do everything in our power to make you happy. Visit WyattNorth.com for more information. Please feel free to contact us with any questions or comments. We welcome your feedback by email at info@WyattNorth.com.

Foreword

One part biography, one part prayer book, The Life and Prayers of Saint Anthony of Padua is an essential book for any Christian.

For centuries Saint Anthony of Padua, Thaumaturgist, Evangelical Doctor of the Church, has been regaled and venerated as a wonder-worker, eminent theologian, and preacher. To him infertile women, sailors, the poor, seekers of lost articles, to name a few, have prayed to intercede. Thousands upon thousands flocked to hear him preach, and witnessed his miraculous deeds.

We hope that with this book, the reader might realize an invitation to call upon Anthony, not just to find lost things, but as a companion in a quest to find a renewed and challenged faith, hope, and love.

The Life of Saint Anthony

"The faithful dweller of the hermitage was sent out into the world and his lips, closed for so long, were opened to proclaim the glory of God." – <u>The Assidua</u>

I. His Life, His Lessons, His Legacy

The Lord anointed his servant, Saint Anthony of Padua, and put a call on a boy's heart to labor for God's kingdom until death. This writing is an attempt to illuminate the many facets of this great saint who, over close to eight centuries since his death, continues to inspire and assist.

Perhaps in this book, among a plethora about Saint Anthony of Padua, the reader might realize an invitation to call upon Anthony, not just to find lost things, but to companion with him/her in a quest to find himself/herself renewed and challenged in faith, hope, and love. What better friend and guide than this servant who demonstrated a remarkable balance between inward piety and study, and full engagement in the world into which God placed him. Although canonized more quickly after his death than any other, S. Anthony would be the first to say that anyone can follow in his footsteps by being contemplatively receptive, biblically attentive, and ready to answer to the cries of the needy.

May such an invitation resound in you as you read again, or for the first time, about the life, lessons, and legacy of this great Catholic Saint, Anthony of Padua.

II. His World

For centuries Saint Anthony of Padua, Thaumaturgist, Evangelical Doctor of the Church, has been regaled and venerated as a wonder-worker, eminent theologian, and preacher. To him infertile women, sailors, the poor, seekers of lost articles, to name a few, have prayed to intercede.

Thousands upon thousands flocked to hear him preach, and witnessed his miraculous deeds. To address S. Anthony's life and work apart from the place and time in which God placed him would be to ignore that he, like all of us, is in part a product of the significant moments and culture of his day. Unlike ordinary mortals, however, Saint Anthony of Padua, by God's grace, was able to fully engage himself in the world for God's purposes, tirelessly performing deeds sacred and profane, that left his God-forsaken world a better place.

The span of thirty-seven years of S. Anthony's earthly sojourn (1195-1231) fell within The High Middle Ages, a time marked by population growth not seen before or again until the 1900's, an expansion that shifted every arena in which humans operated. Consider the events unfolding in the land of his birth, Portugal, then referred to as the Iberian Peninsula.

Over centuries Lisbon, where **Ferdinand Martins de Bulhoes** (S. Anthony's baptismal name) was born, was a European coastal attraction to every sea-faring conqueror from as far north as the Vikings of Scandinavia, to as far away as the Moors. These vastly varied cultures left their footprints on Portugal's shores, altering forever the demographic and secular and religious culture of S. Anthony's homeland. Only four decades before his birth, within the seven-centuries-long Reconquista (the struggle of Christians to conquer the Iberian Peninsula from Islamic kingdoms), knights took Lisbon back from Muslim control to restore her to Christianity. This localized struggle reflected events in the wider theatre, the crusades, the ongoing fight between Muslims and

Christians for control of Jerusalem, the spiritual epicenter of both religions.

S. Anthony would personally encounter the atrocities of the crusades as an adult, and his family's fidelity to the Church would insure his early Christian formation. With the cross-fertilization of cultures in Lisbon, where Ferdinand spent the first fifteen years of his life, it's likely he might have played with the children whose forebears came from faraway lands, vastly different than his own. Perhaps he stood by and watched Christian statues and churches rise from the litter where mosques had been razed in the struggle for Christian dominance.

Four Popes led the Church over S. Anthony's brief span of years on earth. Most likely the greatest influence on his thinking and ministry was Pope Innocent III - although it was Pope Gregory IX who put S. Anthony "on the map" - whose ability to influence politics in nations across Europe established his papacy as the most renowned of the Middle Ages. Pope Innocent gave audience to and authorized the mendicant order that S. Anthony joined after his eight years as Canons Regular of St. Augustine. The Order of Friars Minor, established by St. Francis of Assisi, was attractive to Pope Innocent for its commitment to a life of obedience, simplicity and chastity.

Not unaware of the slovenly and self-indulgent ways of clergy and laity, The Pope acknowledged those who were loyal to the Church and its doctrine. Innocent III's thoughtful and prolific writings during his Papacy and during retirement, and the seventy canons he issued at "The Great Council" (the Fourth Lateran Council) in 1215, no doubt, influenced S. Anthony's moral and doctrinal theology, especially with regards to the Eucharist. The Pope's canon on the Doctrine of Transubstantiation established the belief that the bread and the wine are the actual body and blood of our Lord Jesus.

III. Turning Points

T he following provide important turning points in the life of Saint Anthony.

<u>1195</u>: S. Anthony's genealogy is uncertain, even though fifteenth-century accounts attribute his father's parentage to a renowned naval commander of the First crusade and to nobility on his mother's side. Ferdinand Martins de Bulhoes was born and baptized in Lisbon, Spain to noble parents, August 15, 1195.

An education in the liberal arts was the privilege of boys of nobility. Girls who wanted to learn to read and write had to join a convent or be schooled at home. Bishops (religious educators) and monks taught in the cathedral school Ferdinand attended, the school attached to the Cathedral of Lisbon.

He likely received a classical education with course offerings not unlike a liberal arts education today. Math, music, geometry, rhetoric, logic, and astronomy, with a strong serving of Latin, constituted the typical cathedral school curriculum of his day. Knowledge of Latin was critical to understand the Mass and to unlock the Bible and ancient texts, and no doubt Ferdinand, a natural intellect, studied hard and learned well.

<u>1210</u>: It would be years later before Ferdinand's keen intellect would be discovered and unleashed for God's purposes, but one might imagine the spark of God was lit in his fertile mind and heart at a very young age. The first biography of S. Anthony, written just after his death, <u>The Assidua</u> referred to Ferdinand's longing for depth of understanding and contemplation, compelling him, allegedly against his parent's wishes, to enter (at age 15 or 16) the Augustinian Priory of Saint Vincent.

In 1210 he joined the Canons Regular, residing just outside the city walls. Ferdinand left his boyhood home to join a community of clerics, or priests, who performed priestly duties in local parishes, and lived in community, sharing their things in common as instructed by the rule of Saint Augustine of Hippo. As a mere boy, a tenth-grader in the USA, what might Ferdinand's daily life have been like as a new Canons Regular?

1212: Tradition has it he was so often visited by family and friends his superiors transferred him to the Augustinian house in Coimbra, the mother house of Portugal, where he continued to immerse himself in study and prayer. The Assidua testified to S. Anthony's diligence as a student of books and of holy pursuits.

1220: The harsh realities of the wider world came knocking, kindling in Ferdinand a desire to take quite literally Jesus' exhortation to the ruler who knew his lessons well, but for one: the requirement to sell all he had and distribute it to the poor "and follow me." (Luke 18.22)

When the relics of five Franciscan martyrs were paraded around the city and exhibited at Ferdinand's monastery (They had preached Christ to the Muslims in Morocco, in spite of warning and were eventually tortured and beheaded), Ferdinand was overcome by great zeal to be a martyr for the Faith. Not far from the monastery where he lived, a group of Franciscan friars crossed Ferdinand's path while begging for alms. Ferdinand told them of his desire to be a martyr for the cause of Christ. He had also been inspired by a sermon from Mathew 10:9, "take no gold, no silver, no copper in your belt" to devote his whole life to austerity and simplicity in the example of the young order's founder, Brother Francis.

Not long after his encounter, the friars returned to Ferdinand's convent with the humble robes of the Order of Friars Minor. Probably not without earnest deliberation, the Canons Regular released Ferdinand the Augustinian to become Anthony the Franciscan. His wish to embark for Morocco came true, but God had other plans for him than to be his martyr in North Africa. He was very ill while in Morocco. When setting sail for Portugal, the ship was blown off course. After several months at sea, an ill

Anthony and comrades landed in Sicily, a strange land and far from the home to which he would never return.

Needing succor, Anthony was taken in by brother friars in Messina. Still ill, he attended the General Chapter meeting called the Pentecost Chapter of Mats of the Friars Minor in Assisi. Anthony's gifts and experience went unnoticed; his first biographer testified that the humble Anthony never mentioned his achievements as a scholar and servant. His only desire was to follow the Christ of the cross.

As an unknown at the meeting with nothing to occupy him, S. Anthony felt compelled to request time in silence and seclusion to do penance and practice the disciplines of the Franciscan life. He appealed to the Franciscan Provincial of Romagna to be permitted this time. Glad to have someone celebrate Mass for the brothers in Forli, the Provincial allowed S. Anthony to go north to a hermitage in Montepaelo.

1222: Just as the Lord spent time in the wilderness before entering the public arena to preach, teach, and heal, so did S. Anthony. The ten months of seclusion, prayer, and deep rest at Montepaolo, ended quite abruptly. He was invited to travel with Franciscan and Dominican friends to Forli for an ordination. No one was prepared to preach and no one was willing to speak unprepared. It was assumed that S. Anthony was untrained, so he was invited to speak a simple message. Everything changed when he opened his mouth. Not so much because of the polish of his delivery, but because of his grasp of the subtleties of the Scriptures and doctrine, and the spirit that emanated from him, it was impossible to deny his anointing and his holiness.

1224: S. Anthony's public witness had begun. Soon thereafter Francis ordered him to teach theology to the friars preparing for priesthood and to evangelize the countryside.

This letter, supposedly, came from S. Francis to his brother, Anthony.

> *To Brother Anthony, my bishop, Brother Francis sends his greetings. It is my Pleasure that thou teach theology to the brethren, provided, however, that As the Rule prescribes, the spirit of prayer and devotion may not Be extinguished.*

(Dal-Gal, Niccolò (1907). "St. Anthony of Padua. The Catholic Encyclopedia. Robert Appleton Company.)

This little quote offers significant insight into the influence of S. Francis on the spirituality of S. Anthony. Before beginning his ministry between northern Italy and southern France as lecturer, but mostly as preacher and miracle worker, he spent time with the noted Abbot, Thomas Gallo to whom, legend has it, S. Anthony appeared after his death.

1224-1226: In these years S. Anthony spent his time in Le-Puy and in the province of Limousin, France as Custos Provincial, an official Franciscan appointment that gave him oversight of the friars and voice in the General Chapter. Le-Puy was a popular pilgrimage site for dignitaries as august as Constantine. Authentic accounts of his many miracles come from this period of his life spent in Limousin, which is all we know of his time there. Upon the death of S. Francis, October 3, 1226, S. Anthony returned to Italy; there, he was elected Minister Provincial of Emilia.

1230: S. Anthony resigned his office at General Chapter of Assisi to devote more time to preaching and to establish residence at the convent he founded in Padua.

<u>1231</u>: This year was the year of S. Anthony's biggest transition, and perhaps the biggest year of transformation for his followers. After he preached during Lent on reconciliation and penance, there were not enough priests in the region to hear confessions. His prophetic admonishments of the unjust practices caused municipality officials to pass a law in Padua to relieve debt for those who couldn't pay. During this time many miracles were witnessed at his hand.

Recognizing that his life was coming to an end, S. Anthony retired to Camposampiero, about thirty miles north of Padua. Craving to be secluded and silent, he asked Count Tiso, who had constructed a hermitage there, to build him a tree hut in the branches of a walnut tree. There, he spent a good bit of his time in the last months of his life. A chapel called the Shrine of the Walnut tree marks that place.

<u>June 13, 1231</u>: S. Anthony, climbed down from his tree where he had placed himself, not on the earth, and not quite in heaven. Feeling ill, he asked to be taken back to Padua. Too sick to make it all the way, the caravan stopped in Vercelli, some say the Convent of the Poor Clares at Arcella, where he was given last rights and sang a song. An apparition of the Lord encouraged his surrender into the eternal arms of his first and only Love.

<u>May 30, 1232</u>: Pope Gregory IX, having heard of his miracles and after hearing S. Anthony preach in Rome, entered S. Anthony into the Calendar of Saints at the Cathedral of Spoleto.

<u>1263</u>: S. Anthony's relics were transferred to a basilica the city of Padua constructed in his honor.

<u>January 16, 1946</u>: Although it is believed Pope Gregory pronounced S. Anthony Doctor of the Church, it was Pope Pius

XII in his encyclical letter *Exulta Lusitania felix* where "Doctor of the Church" was formally declared.

June 13, 1994: Pope John Paul II delivered a message on the eighth centenary of S. Anthony's birth.

January 16, 1996: Pope John Paul II delivered his open letter to the Franciscan Minister General to celebrate the 50th anniversary of the proclamation of S.Anthony as Doctor of the Church.

III. Evangelist and Preacher

When you think of those two words, **evangelist** and **preacher** what meaning do they evoke?

Perhaps they evoke images of the television evangelist's tearful pleas for more money. Perhaps the word "preacher" makes us think of theatre-sized screens in the sanctuary on which moving images momentarily draw our eyes from our iPhones and prompt us to be more diligent in prayer and mission.

Like today, priests and laity in S. Anthony's day could be found along all points of the spectrum, from lazy and insipid— to downright heretical— to dynamic, faithful, and fruitful. Temptation and apostasy are not time-sensitive; sins and departure from true Faith have tempted and taken root since Adam and Eve. But among those called to preach and witness the good news of our Lord there were none to approach S. Anthony, none who warranted the uncontested and immediate acclaim and rank of sainthood.

What set him apart would no doubt be the decision of his sovereign Lord to embody himself in his servant Anthony to bring "poor sinners" to himself through healing, preaching, teaching, and signs and wonders. But S. Anthony had to cooperate. He had to be a clear channel of that grace.

Jesus said that one could distinguish the false prophets ("who come to you in sheep's clothing but inwardly are ravenous wolves") from his own prophets by the fruits they bore (Matthew 7:15-16). Could the incredible bounty of transformed humans and institutions wrought from S. Anthony's preaching and evangelizing be in part due to his grounding in Scripture? Could it be his understanding that the message was the messenger?

And this is why S. Francis, after hearing of S. Anthony's first sermon preached at the ordination in Forli, ordered him to instruct the friars and to begin preaching and evangelizing in northern Italy. The Holy Spirit pouring through him created a natural attraction to listeners, but that holiness was forged, in part, by S. Anthony's willingness to commit himself to prayer (influenced by Francis) and assiduous study of the Bible (influenced by Augustine of Hippo).

In 1996, on the occasion of the fiftieth anniversary of the proclamation of S. Anthony as Doctor of the Church, Pope John Paul II wrote an open letter to the Franciscan's Minister General. In the letter he elaborated on the gifts of S. Anthony, saying that because he "beheld the true splendor of the triune God through prayer and contemplation, and further from the riches of his mind and in communion with the church, he transmitted this to others."

In that same address Pope John Paul II affirmed that S. Anthony's "assiduous evangelization and indefatigable preaching" came from "the sacraments, primarily from penance and the Eucharist....Anthony was not a half-hearted preacher but a man of energy and charisma who brought not only learning and holiness to his task but great strength of purpose."

On the eight-hundredth centenary of S. Anthony's birth, June 13, 1994, Pope John Paul II extolled the saint's preaching by attesting to his use of scholarly tools he had available at the time, and by speaking the same language as his hearers, measures which helped to assure that Gospel values were received by the popular culture of his day. S. Anthony did not discriminate among his hearers. He would just as soon proclaim the Lordship of Christ to a poor beggar as to the Pope. It is said he preached so convincingly at the synod at Bourges, Archbishop de Sully was moved to make a sincere amends. His exhortations inspired changes in unjust laws that impacted prisoners and the poor.

But, to those who had distorted the true gospel, he was known as "Hammer of Heretics" and there were plenty of them to go around. S. Anthony understood Paul's teachings that the Gospel of Christ is a proclamation over and against all false gods, not an alternative. All will be measured against the plumb line of God's Kingdom in Jesus Christ. No other god could be entertained, but the Lord Jesus who, through his servant S. Anthony, performed the same as He.

The power of oral proclamation was indeed the charism by which S. Anthony reaped abundant harvest. A powerful voice, a steel trap mind, a monolithic memory, and there was yet another ingredient to his evangelical power. Remember the young Ferdinand who wanted to be a martyr? To evangelize reaches beyond just oral proclamation of the gospel. The Latin for "witness" is *martyria*; evangelism is nothing less than following the way of the crucified.

The expression: "You may be the only Bible others will ever read," certainly applied to S. Anthony. When S. Anthony spoke, especially to the poor, he didn't ride in on a fancy carriage, speak words, then leave. He walked among the poor as a poor man. He was his sermon, his Bible. He might have quoted Apostle Paul who said to the Romans, "I have *fully* preached the gospel." (Romans 15:19)

IV. Thaumaturgist, Worker of Miracles

If testimonies to miracles in the New Testament were removed, half of the book would be eliminated. Through miracles the Lord convinced onlookers he was no mere teacher of morals, nor just another option among a pantheon of gods; he was the one who tamed the seas, healed the lame, the one whose conquest of death gave hope eternal that the Light would never be overcome. (John 1)

"The mark of a true apostle," said Paul to the Corinthians (I Corinthians 12:12) "are signs, wonders, and miracles." Audiences hearing the good news, in any era, can be deaf and their loyalties drawn to any fad that captivates them in the moment. Why should one, often suddenly and dramatically, accept the Lord of Life? To Jesus and many of his Apostles, God supplied the power to perform signs and wonders. When the spoken word was not enough, said St. Luke in the Book of Acts, miracles "confirmed the word" (Acts 14:3).

These were not magic tricks conjured by sorcery, but the awesome power of the sovereign Creator of the Universe who could supply or withhold that power. This chapter features only a few of copious miracles performed during S. Anthony's life and after his death. Whether the stuff of legend, or passed down through the centuries from reliable witnesses, the miracles of S. Anthony set him apart, even among saints.

One can easily find exhaustive lists and accounts of miracles performed by S. Anthony. In 1899 Joseph A. Keller, in The Miracles of St. Anthony of Padua compiled a detailed and extensive accounting of miracles. Keller's list was modernized by Rev. Brother Sean Bradley in 2008. These few are drawn from Keller's list, and are the ones most often spoken of, and are considered authentic

Why S. Anthony is implored to find lost items:

Certainly, S. Anthony was crestfallen to discover that his Psalter with copious notes he used to teach theology to the younger friars was gone. Books of any kind were precious and expensive to purchase. A younger brother was fed up with monastic life, and it is said he left with S. Anthony's book. Being the man he was, S. Anthony prayed for the boy whom he suspected and that the Psalter would be returned. At the moment of his prayer the young brother was encountered by a terrifying apparition that threatened death if he didn't return the stolen property. The boy obeyed and returned the Psalter to S. Anthony and rejoined the order. The book resides at the Franciscan monastery in Bologna.

Centuries after S. Anthony's death a lay Capuchin Brother had misplaced his prized rosary. When the string broke the beads went everywhere. One was missing and he prayed to S. Anthony for help. To his amazement a tiny ant crawled towards him carrying the missing bead.

Even the fish listen:

> *Come, ye senseless fishes of the deep, and by your attention to the word of your God and mine, put to shame these men, who in their blindness and hardness of heart refuse to hear it.* – S. Anthony of Padua

With heresy on the rise at rates unseen before in northern Italy and southern France, Francis ordered S. Anthony to assert his great gifts to convert the infidels. In Rimini S. Anthony preached to a faithful few, and upon learning of the power of this man of God, the heretics were determined to get rid of him. Aware of the magnitude of the task ahead of him, S. Anthony went away to pray and fast in solitude to prepare to change hearts. At the Marecchia River he prayed the prayer above; fish came in huge schools to hear the Word preached. S. Anthony's enemies were spying on him and many witnessed the fish heeding the powerful sermon preached as if the fish were his congregation.

To you it has been given to save His prophet Jonas; to cure His blind servant. Tobias; to be the food of the penitent; to procure for the Saviour of [18] mankind and His disciples the tribute money due to Caesar; it was after His Resurrection by eating of your flesh He proved He was truly risen from the dead; it was over your heads He walked on the sea, and after the great draught of fishes, He called His apostles fishers of men. – S. Anthony of Padua

The fish seemed to cling to every word and the bystanders were so moved, many repented, confessed, and became followers of Christ. By view of this miracle the city of Rimini was expunged of heretics.

His appearance with the Christ Child:

Tito Borghese, Count of Campo San Pietro, lived at the monastery in Arcella not far from Padua. S. Anthony often stayed the night there and Tito made it his business to record the activities of S. Anthony, whom he revered. One night he noticed a shaft of light emanating from S. Anthony's quarters. He observed through the keyhole S. Anthony holding a baby. It was the Christ Child. When the two men talked later, S. Anthony implored the Count never to tell anyone what had happened. Tito kept the secret until after S. Anthony's death.

The broken goblet:

This miracle happened (c. 1226) when S. Anthony and his companion were traveling in the Provence to a meeting of the General Chapter. They stopped at a home where a pious woman lived. She wanted to give the guests every honor, so she borrowed a valuable goblet from a neighbor. The companion broke the goblet. The woman forgot to shut off the wine barrel tap and the wine ran out. S. Anthony's prayers restored the broken goblet and the wine. The two men left town quickly as not to be waylaid by crowds.

Heart full of treasure:

While in Florence, S. Anthony wanted to impress the listeners about the evils of usery. A very rich man who had profited in ways that S. Anthony abhorred, had died. S. Anthony preached at his funeral, saying that because of his greed, the deceased had condemned his soul to hell, because his treasures in life were his gold and possessions.

> *To prove the truth of my assertion you need only go and look at the chest of money, which, for the short time he lived on earth, was the joy and god of his heart, and you will find there that heart lying under his gold. For the Son of God Himself has declared, 'Where your treasure is there also is your heart.'* – St. Anthony of Padua

The mourners did just that and to their astonishment found the heart of the deceased in the money chest. Still not convinced, they insisted on opening the chest cavity of the Userer. There, they found no heart. Could any sermon on Luke 12:34 ("Where your heart is, there your treasure will be also") be more dramatically illustrated?

Nothing is known of S. Anthony's time spent in Limousin when he was Custos Provincial, except for the series of miracles he performed there.

- He was preaching in Limoges and he remembered he was to sing one of the lessons. He bi-located, at once singing in the choir and preaching in the pulpit.

- For a servant who was bringing food from a benefactor of the convent he had founded at Brive, he made the rain stop. Again, in Limoges, he made the rain stop while he was preaching on the square.

- In a sermon at St. Julien he told the congregation that the devil would make the pulpit fall, but that no one would be injured. This happened. (Dal-Gal)

For almost eight-hundred years people have prayed for help finding lost things, among countless other requests of the beneficent S. Anthony.

V. Evangelical Doctor of the Church

Even though Doctors of the Church had been promoted earlier, it was Pope Benedict (1740-1758) who established the benchmark for the lofty distinction. One must be officially designated by the papacy which, as of this writing, has recognized 33 doctors (*docere* = Latin for 'to teach') for their holiness and scholarship. Of note, Pope Benedict announced May 10, 2012 that Hildegard of Bingen will be officially promoted to Doctor of the Church, although not canonized, on October 7, 2012. Essentially, each of these Doctors of the Church is noted for their contributions to theology and doctrine.

S. Anthony was pronounced a *Doctor Evangelicus* (Evangelizing Doctor) in 1946, the 29th Doctor in the list of 33, by Pope Pius XII. He wrote in his *Exulta*: "Anthony is revealed as most skilled in sacred scripture, as a remarkable theologian of the teachings of our faith and as an exceptional teacher and master in ascetical and mystical subjects."

To delve in depth into S. Anthony's doctrine and theology and the principle influences, would warrant an entire book. No doubt those influences were his teacher at the Cathedral school, and his reading, discussion and debate on the highlights and subtleties of many of the philosophical and theological classics and biblical commentaries as a Canons Regular.

The two who most influenced his thinking and piety were St. Augustine and St. Francis while S. Anthony was a Canons Regular in Portugal, and Friars Minor in Italy and France, respectively. While it was St. Augustine who refined S. Anthony's thinking on biblical interpretation, doctrine and theology, it was Brother Francis whose literal approach to the Gospel, and Rule guided him in matters of communal life, possessions, preaching, and prayer.

St. Augustine's teachings:

As S. Anthony's teacher, St. Augustine, among the four great Doctors of the Western Church, was staggeringly prolific; a foundational read for S. Anthony surely would have been Augustine's four books in _De doctrina christiana_, On Christian Doctrine, written in 397 and 426. These books describe how to interpret and teach the Bible, which of course was of central concern for S. Anthony whose call was to preach and teach, using the Bible as his foundational text. Augustine's books from On Christian Doctrine were the tool that Christendom applied to confront paganism in Augustine's day; likewise they instructed S. Anthony for teaching the true Faith to the friars, heretics, and believers alike. Some of Augustine's teachings from On Christian Doctrine are discernible in S. Anthony's teaching and the way he lived his life.

- Sound interpretation of the Scriptures is marked by love, charity, knowledge, reason and eloquence. (Book One)

- The steps to wisdom when interpreting Scripture are: fear of God, faith, knowledge, strength, good counsel, purity of heart. (Book Two)

- For best understanding, one must commit the Bible to memory. (Book Two)

- Eloquence in preaching is in service to wisdom. (Book Four)

- The preacher's life is his sermon. (Book Four)

- Humility and prayer are essential for wise and eloquent preaching. (Book Four)

On matters of doctrine: the nature of God, the divinity and humanity of Christ, the Eucharist, Mary, salvation and resurrection, the Church, piety and prayer, St.Augustine was of course prolific and profound. It is beyond the scope of this book to delve into the complexities and subtle points of Augustinian systematics.

St. Francis' teachings:

After his conversion, "the servant of Christ, seeing that the number of his friars was gradually increasing, wrote for himself and for him a form of life in simple words, laying as its irremovable foundation the observance of the holy Gospel and adding a few other things which seemed necessary for uniformity of life." (See The Writings of St. Francis of Assisi, Trans. by Paschal Robinson, 1905.) Upon Pope Innocent III's approval of what came to be known as the first Rule, St. Francis and his friars were officially deemed Church loyalist, and not heretics as once suspected. The brotherhood grew so quickly while S. Anthony was among them, many revisions to the rule were made between 1209 and 1223, but the essential essence remained unchanged. Some points of the Rule that echoed in Anthony's teaching.

- On working with "Saracens and other Infidels", i.e. working among heretics (16): "The brothers who go may conduct themselves in two ways spiritually among them. One way is not to make disputes or contentions; but let them...confess(ing) themselves to be Christians. The other way is...announce the Word of God, that they may believe in Almighty God...and that they should be baptized and be made Christians, because, 'unless a man be born again of water and the Holy Ghost, he cannot enter into the kingdom of God'....If they should persecute you in one city flee to another. 'But he that shall persevere to the end, he shall be saved.'"

- That all the Brothers must live in a Catholic way, i.e. fidelity to the Church (19): "But if anyone should err from the Catholic faith and life in word or in deed, and will not amend, let him be altogether expelled from our fraternity."

- "But now, after having renounced the world, we have nothing else to do but to be solicitous, to follow the will of God, and to please Him." (22)

- The nature of the trinity (23): "Let us therefore desire nothing else, wish for nothing else, and let nothing please and delight us except our Creator and Redeemer, and Savior, the only true God, who is full of good, all good, entire good, the true and supreme good, merciful and kind, gentle and sweet, who alone is holy, just, true and upright, who alone is benign, pure, and clean, from whom, and through whom, and in whom is all mercy." (P. Robinson)

S. Anthony is the only Doctor of the Church who bears the title with the qualifier, "Evangelical". Often we think of the professor sequestered in an ivory tower, deeply absorbed in reading and learning, and when speaking, he/she speaks in some esoteric language that only those in his/her discipline can understand. From the many testimonies of the brotherhood's passion for evangelism, S. Anthony, with the love of Christ, would gladly sacrifice life and limb that one might be saved.

S. Anthony's sole purpose was to touch others' lives with the good news of the Gospel. Leaving great writings was not his modus operandi as an evangelist, like for so many of his colleagues. He was his "book" about the mercy and grace of God, and when people read him and listened to him speak they were changed forever. S. Anthony spoke volumes.

VI. The Saint

Before the Catholic Church established and formalized procedures to authenticate a believer for sainthood, earliest Christians venerated men and women who died for confessing Christ (martyrs), and people of extraordinary faith (Confessors).

Early written testimonies, alters at the tomb, and ceremonies were ways believers venerated and memorialized the most faithful. As early as the second and third centuries diptychs (*sacrae tabulae*) - read as part of liturgy - recorded the church faithful, living and dead, who served and sacrificed in all capacities: church members, the baptized, higher Church officials, martyrs, saints, benefactors, celebrants, and the Blessed Virgin.

The diptychs fell out of use around S. Anthony's time in the West, and were precursors to ecclesiastical calendars (into which Pope Gregory IX entered S. Anthony's name) and martyrologies. One need not look further than the great works of art, extant writings, and liturgy, to know who many of these earliest bold believers were. By the third century martyrs were placed under strict scrutiny and examination to determine the authenticity of claims that they had died for the Faith and were worthy of the title and of veneration.

As unregulated and impulsive claims for sainthood became a problem, in 1234 the Church implemented a formal process for canonization. It was St. Gregory IX, who declared S. Anthony a saint, who desired a more formal process. Over the centuries rules and procedures leading to canonization have adjusted and changed. In 1983, Pope John Paul II created controversy when he relaxed procedures. It seemed unfair that those who passed muster after rigorous and long drawn-out examinations would be compared to those for whom the bar was and is now lowered. There are some who refuse to acknowledge anyone canonized after 1983.

Even so, the investigation for sainthood must prove that the candidate, by his/her virtues, miracles, and fidelity to the Church, is in heaven and not in purgatory. Then the faithful may look to the saint as an example and inspiration in holy living; they may pray to the saint to intercede on their behalf, and remember them when mentioned in Mass.

In either case, the following is the process that S. Anthony would be subjected to today. Would he pass muster?

- To allow for greater objectivity the candidate can't be evaluated until five years after death. (S. Anthony was canonized within one year of his death.)

- The Bishop of the diocese initiates the investigation of the person who has "fame of sanctity" or "fame of martyrdom."

 (S. Anthony joined the Friars Minor because he wanted to follow in the example of the brothers who martyred themselves in Morocco. The Lord had another plan.)

 The "Congregation for the Causes of the Saints" receives an authenticated sealed letter testifying to the orthodoxy of the candidate's writings, preaching, and teaching (they are consistent with Catholic teachings) and to special favors or miracles that occurred through the candidate's intercession. (Pope Gregory IX had no such gate keepers, but the evidence for S. Anthony's orthodoxy demonstrated in his preaching and teaching, and his miracles were irrefutable.)

- When the Congregation accepts the candidate his/her works of charity and virtuosity "with heroism" are further investigated. (S. Anthony's entire life was solely devoted to Christ and his commission to "go into all the world" and to the rules of St. Frances, based in Scripture, that one should see Christ in the most marginal of society. No one could argue that S. Anthony's charity, his selflessness, his sacrifice were of heroic proportions.)

- "A devil's advocate" is appointed to find "holes" in the candidate's "holiness." (S. Anthony surely had enemies, but none who could poke holes in the verity of his signs and wonders or in his purity, faith, and wisdom.)

- If the "general promoter of the faith" cannot tarnish the candidate then he/she is declared Venerable.

- More investigations and interviews are performed to authenticate at least one miracle from intercession. Mother Theresa's examination is at this stage. (See part IV of this book)

- The candidate is beatified and may be venerated with certain restrictions, geographical or familial. (St. Anthony's reputation spread quickly beyond Padua and the regions where he served. Then and today his veneration is global. See part VII of this book.)

- The Pope authorizes liturgies, prayers, and divine offices in honor of the beatified.

- One more step: Another miracle must be verified due to intercession. (To this day believers testify of special favors granted by praying to S. Anthony.)

- After all this the Pope receives the candidate's file and makes the final decision to declare the faithful a saint. (In S. Anthony's day the process of canonization was rather arbitrary. So quickly after his death - within one year - was he deemed a saint, he is often referred to as the "fast Saint".)

It can take centuries to be declared a saint. Pope Benedict IX was so convinced of his sanctity and fidelity to the true Faith, he inscribed S. Anthony on Pentecost, 1232 in the Calendar of Saints at the Cathedral in Spoleto Pope Gregory was his own examining body, declaring in the Bull of canonization that he knew the Franciscan brother and heard him preach in Rome, and was so struck by his depth of biblical knowledge he exclaimed, "Ark of the Covenant" place where the Hebrews contained their holiest item, The Torah, and believed Yaweh resided there.

To examine the lists of Catholic Saints is to discover that God does not discriminate as to how they serve: as kings, or popes, martyrs, confessors, priests, or as poor evangelists like S. Anthony.

VII: His Veneration

Memorializing and honoring loved ones with a physical marker, ritual, or celebration is as old as humanity itself. The Catholic Church established such rituals to venerate martyrs and saints as far back as the first century; extant documents speak of people giving homage to the remains (relics) of martyrs at their burial sites. By the third century the Eucharist was celebrated at the tombs of the martyrs.

When Constantine came to power in the fourth century cathedrals and churches were built over tombs of martyrs and saints. A relic of the saint or martyr - literally a part of the saint's body, usually tissue or bone - provided a connection to the one being venerated, and also lent authority and sanctity to the places where the relics were placed. It is a temptation to deify the symbol that points to that person; the devout are duly warned. Yet, according to St. Thomas Aquinas, to ignore them would to miss out on their capacity to "excite to love."

By S. Anthony's day, rituals, liturgies, feast days, structures, and relics were well established means for veneration. S. Anthony requested he be buried in the Church of Santa Maria in Padua. The friars, pilgrims, and the townspeople began work immediately building a basilica in his honor. When the second phase was completed in 1263, and when the Franciscans met for their general chapter, S. Anthony's body was transferred to the first site of his veneration, what today is known as the Basilica of St. Frances Padua, in Padua, Italy. The story goes that his coffin was opened in order to remove relics to be placed in other churches. Except for his tongue, his body was completely decomposed.

It was then that St. Bonaventure, with his heart full of admiration, prayed aloud:

O blessed tongue, you have always praised the Lord and led others to praise him! Now we can clearly see how great indeed have been your merits before God. (From the Basilica of St. Anthony of Padua)

It is said that parts of S. Anthony's body were conserved, namely his tongue, and wrapped in a crimson cloth and placed in a small box within a larger one.

Of note, anticipating S. Anthony's 800th birthday, officials opened his tomb in 1995 to take and distribute relics. The Franciscan Friars of the Province of S. Anthony of America (in Ellicott City, MD) were given a relic and the reliquary that contains, along with 13 original paintings marking significant points in the saint's life, by the Friars of the Province of St. Anthony in Padua. The Province (where the official US Shrine of S. Anthony is located since 2004) placed the relic in the chapel in a special ceremony held in 2000. Pilgrims are invited to join their pilgrimage held on S. Anthony's feast day, June 13.

S. Anthony interceded for so many in their time of need, that he is venerated as patron saint of a vast variety of groups: sailors, American Indians, pregnant women, barren women, elderly, fishermen, travelers, to name a few. Most notably he is venerated as patron saint of lost items. It seems only fitting – even though he is honored the world throughout by Catholics and non-Catholics alike – that anyone for whom S. Anthony has shown special favor would give thanks by offering an ex voto, Latin for "from my vow." When Anthony intercedes with the results prayed for, the recipient of the blessing promises to offer public thanks by placing a small painting, waxen image, a stamped metal or brass piece, or a note in writing in the church. Perhaps one of the most elaborate and expensive ex votos ever offered to S. Anthony was by a very wealthy Portuguese prince who badly wanted a son to inherit his riches. His gratitude was so great when he was granted his desire he had a silver statue cast in the image and weight of the baby prince. He wanted to be so sure that the statue got to S. Anthony's basilica in Padua, he appealed to the Pope to deliver it. The ex voto is there to this day.

Thank offerings mentioned above are made to all saints, but the one that is unique to S. Anthony is the offering in thanksgiving of St. Anthony's Bread. The term "St. Anthony's Bread" denotes thanksgiving for any time S. Anthony has restored a lost item, or healed someone, or restored a person to hope or faith. The tradition began when a woman in Toulon, France vowed she would give bread to the poor if S. Anthony would help her get into her house after she'd lost her keys. He granted her wish. The tradition of making a loaf of bread the size of the one on whose behalf the intercession was successful, or preparing small loaves for distribution to congregants and to the poor, is widely practiced among Catholics, especially on S. Anthony's feast day, June 13.

In S. Anthony's home, Lisbon, a feast day holiday and marriages happen in his honor, marriages because he has been known to reconcile couples. In southern India, Uvari, a wooden statue of the saint is enshrined. It is said to have cured a crew of sailors from cholera. A national shrine in Shri Lanka draws pilgrims of all faiths from around the world. In Brazil he is counted as a General of the Army.

Great works of art, magnificent cathedrals, symphonies, and elaborate ceremonies and liturgies express the honor and gratitude of the faithful to the saint. Artists as famous as El Greco and Titian have portrayed S. Anthony's miracles and his attributes on canvass. He is one of the most featured saints in art, often portrayed holding the Christ Child, holding a book, bread or a lily. "The Mass for St. Anthony of Padua" was composed in the fifteenth century by Guillaume Du Fay and is still being reproduced and sold.

Countless prayers (many of his own included), liturgies, masses, and hymns have been prayed, sung, and celebrated over the centuries to venerate Saint Anthony. Just like on the day he died, children cry out and bells ring in the streets to celebrate his life and legacy, almost eight hundred years later.

VIII: Model for 21st Century Catholics

Catholics in every century have been and are seduced by the voices of culture and by undisciplined appetites, addictions, and countless distractions. God knows this. Among other things, God brings people, even His own son, to show his children how to live a faithful, obedient life, and to invite us to be restored and redeemed through faith and practice.

S. Anthony is one person God blessed to be an eternal blessing to the human and non-human family. In the saint's honor one can casually recite "Tony, tony turn around, something's lost and must be found," or pray the novenas of the nine/thirteen Tuesdays and be done.

But what of the person who inspired the liturgies, the artwork, the music, the sculpture, the churches and cathedrals, the prayers of intercession? In a culture that is plugged in and tuned out, there could be no better time to befriend someone who knew God so intimately and offered charity so willingly.

In S. Anthony Catholics have a wonderful model. For his immersion in Scripture, his disciplines of silence and separation from the world, and return to the world to serve, his virtues and Christ-likeness grew. "But I'm no saint," you protest. The following represent the ways of S. Anthony that one can follow in his/her everyday life.

Acts of Charity:

Countless charities exist in S. Anthony's honor. The order of the Friars Minor (the Franciscans) inspired him in large part because of the brothers' commitment to living in simple poverty among the poor. No, most of us are not called to live a mendicant lifestyle, stripped of the comforts of home like S. Anthony, but this does not preclude making choices that both symbolize and embody charity. For example, one could choose to fast from shopping, or de-clutter and give good cast-offs to charity, or down-size living quarters, or volunteer one hour a month at a soup kitchen, or bake bread to distribute on S. Anthony's Feast day.

One could see "poverty" in ways other than material. Sicknesses of spirit, loss of hope, loneliness, all are forms of poverty. Visiting a lonely shut-in, reconciling with an enemy, giving money to a favorite charity, mentoring a child of a poor single-parent, praying for victims of war, famine, disease - and the list goes on - are acts of charity that don't require taking vows, wearing a scratchy tunic, or walking everywhere.

Perhaps the most insidious form of poverty in our society is self-centeredness and failure of community. Anthony lived in community, with rules and guidelines that required sacrifice and sharing, sensitivity to the needs of the others in the community. Sharing things in common, reciting together the prayer offices, sharing menial tasks, working, playing, and holding each other accountable were part of living together.

Even with sound social teachings, our fast pace and multi-tasking make it nearly impossible for families to share a meal together. More and more the texts and images in our palms and on flat screens steal time and devotion from any form of real or meaningful community and communication. A kind of poverty of intimacy and mutual support and love that characterize life in healthy community, bear consequences yet unseen.

Perhaps the most charitable deed one could do in any given day would be to put away the phone, the laptop, and face one's loved-one, and listen from the heart. Practicing some simple rules of community life based on monastic practices and the ethics of Jesus could also be a valuable act of charity to stem the poverty of loneliness and separation between family members and friends. Returning to the parish church, or joining a prayer group or Bible study fellowship could do much to address the poverty from lack of community in one's own life.

<u>Communion with God</u>:

At heart S. Anthony was a mystic. He longed for the union modeled by the mystical union of the Trinity. Although he was very public in his ministry he craved those times when he could be apart and separate with God. Jesus had an active public ministry too, and he made time to "go to a lonely place" (Matthew 6:6) and pray to the Father. The mystic union between Jesus and God was fashioned from the beginning of creation. Jesus often spoke of the necessity for believers to be joined with him, of making a home together, of vines and branches connected (John 15) because separation meant death. Certainly S. Anthony preached this message.

It was not a stretch for S. Anthony to emulate the teachings of both Augustine and Francis whose model of piety was time given to silence and solitude, meditation, and *lectia divina*, or reflection on Scripture. One sermon believed to be actually preached by S. Anthony, from <u>The Sermons of St. Anthony</u>, Translated by Paul Spilsbury, "A Sermon Preached at the Abbey of St. Martin, Limoges", alludes throughout to mystical union with Christ:

> *So the religious soul finds in the heart of Jesus a secure refuge against the attacks of Satan, and a delightful retreat. But one must not stay at the entrance...she must hasten to the very source from which it springs, into the very innermost sanctuary of the heart of Jesus. There she will find light, peace, and ineffable consolations.*

Steal time to cultivate deeper connections with God, to learn to rest beneath the cross-currents of worry and anxiety, to rest in the heart of Jesus. Centering Prayer practices may be found by finding the websites for the many Christian contemplative organizations that have sprung up in the past twenty years to bring monastic practices to ordinary Christians. A book titled <u>A Retreat with Anthony of Padua: Finding Our Way,</u> by Carol Ann Morrow might be a helpful guideline for a retreat. In this book S. Anthony speaks in first person and invites the reader to take the time to explore what might be lost in himself/herself that needs finding.

It was finding his lost son in the parable in Matthew 15 that led the overjoyed father to sacrifice the best calf. This was as celebration. He had lost his son, and now the lost boy was found. One can imagine that Anthony of Padua, patron saint of lost items is delighted to be called upon for help finding keys, television remotes, and such sundry items.

But perhaps it would please him most to know that Catholics across the world follow in his footsteps by choosing the same simple daily practices of contemplative prayer and acts of charity for the restoration of souls, in Christ.

Prayers by Saint Anthony of Padua

Saint Anthony's Blessing

Behold, the Cross of the Lord!

Begone, all evil powers!
The Lion of the tribe of Judah,
The Root of David, has conquered!
Alleluia, Alleluia!

Prayer to the Holy Spirit

O God, send forth your Holy Spirit into my heart that I may perceive, into my mind that I may remember, and into my soul that I may meditate.

Inspire me to speak with piety, holiness, tenderness and mercy.

Teach, guide and direct my thoughts and senses from beginning to end.

May your grace ever help and correct me, and may I be strengthened now with wisdom from on high, for the sake of your infinite mercy.

Amen.

Prayers to Saint Anthony

Prayer I

Saint Anthony, perfect imitator of Jesus,
who received from God
the special power of restoring lost things,
grant that I may find

(name the lost object)

which has been lost.
At least restore to me peace and tranquility of mind,
the loss of which has afflicted me even more than my material
loss.
To this favour I ask another of you:
that I may always remain in possession of the true good which is
God.
Let me rather lose all things than lose God,
my supreme good.
Let me never suffer the loss of my greatest treasure,
eternal life with God.

Amen

Prayer II

Glorious Saint Anthony, my friend and special protector, I come to you with full confidence in my present necessity. In your overflowing generosity you hear all those who turn to you. Your influence before the throne of God is so effective that the Lord readily grants great favors at your request. Please listen to my humble petition in spite of my unworthiness and sinfulness. Consider only your great and constant love for Jesus and Mary, and my desire for their glory and mercy. I beg you to obtain for me the grace I so greatly need, if it be God's will and for the good of my soul. I place this earnest petition in the care of the little mission children so that they may present it to you along their innocent prayers. Bless me, powerful Saint Anthony, in the name of the Father, and of the Son, and of the Holy Spirit. Amen.

Prayer III

Glorious Saint Anthony, I salute you as a good servant of Christ, and a special friend of God. You once were favored to hold the Christ Child in your arms as you cherished His world in your heart. Today I place all my cares, temptations and anxieties in your hands. I resolve ever to honor you by imitating your example. Powerful patron, model of purity and victor over fleshly impulses, please win for me, and for all devoted to you, perfect purity of body, mind and heart. I promise by my example and counsel to help others to the knowledge, love and service of God. Amen.

Prayer IV

Saint Anthony of Padua, you endured much discouragement in your life before finding your calling. help us to find patience in our own lives, and to trust God to lead us where we need to go. You preached by example; help us show others through example the truth of our faith. Amen.

Prayer V

O Holy Saint Anthony, gentlest of Saints, your love for God and Charity for His creatures, made you worthy, when on earth, to possess miraculous powers. Encouraged by this thought, I implore you to obtain for me [request]. O gentle and loving Saint Anthony, whose heart was ever full of human sympathy, whisper my petition into the ears of the sweet Infant Jesus, who loved to be folded in your arms; and the gratitude of my heart will ever be yours. Amen.

Prayer VI

O good and gentle Saint Anthony, your love of God and concern for His creatures made you worthy, while on earth, to possess miraculous powers. Come to my help in this moment of trouble and anxiety. Your ardent love of God made you worthy to hold the Holy Infant in your arms. Whisper to Him my humble request if it be for the greater glory of God, and the salvation of my soul. Amen.

For Lost Objects

Saint Anthony, when you prayed,

your stolen book of prayers was given back to you.
Pray now for all of us who have lost things precious and dear.
Pray for all who have lost faith,
hope or the friendship of God.
Pray for us who have lost friends or relatives by death.
Pray for all who have lost peace of mind or spirit.
Pray that we may be given new hope, new faith, new love.
Pray that lost things,
needful and helpful to us,
may be returned to our keeping.
Or, if we must continue in our loss,
pray that we may be given Christ's comfort and peace.

Amen.

86270826R00039